TIME
REMAINING

ALSO BY JAMES P. LENFESTEY

Stephen Crane: Selected Poems, editor

Seasons of the Urban Coyote: Essays on Family, Community, and the Search for Peace and Justice

The Uncommon Speech of Paradise: Poems on the Art of Poetry, coeditor

Thirteen September Moons: A Love Story

East Bluff: Mackinac Poems Old & New

A Marriage Book: 50 Years of Poems from a Marriage

If Bees Are Few: A Hive of Bee Poems, editor

Seeking the Cave: A Pilgrimage to Cold Mountain

Earth in Anger: Twenty-Five Poems of Love and Despair for Planet Earth

Robert Bly in This World, coeditor

Low Down and Coming On: A Feast of Delicious and Dangerous Poems about Pigs, editor

A Cartload of Scrolls: 100 Poems in the Manner of T'Ang Dynasty Poet Han-Shan

Into the Goodhue County Jail: Poems to Free Prisoners

The Toothed and Clever World

Han-shan Is the Cure for Warts

Affection for Spiders

Saying Grace: Wisconsin Poems

Odalisque

TIME REMAINING

Body Odes, Praise Songs, Oddities, Amazements

JAMES P. LENFESTEY

MILKWEED EDITIONS

Published 2024 by Milkweed Editions
Printed in Canada
Cover design by Mary Austin Speaker
Cover photo by John F. Walsh Jr., Hearthtone Video
 and Photo, Minneapolis
Author photo by John F. Walsh Jr.
24 25 26 27 28   5 4 3 2 1
First Edition

Library of Congress Cataloging-in-Publication Data

Names: Lenfestey, James P., author.
Title: Time remaining : body odes, praise songs, oddities, amazements / James P. Lenfestey.
Description: First edition. | Minneapolis, Minnesota : Milkweed Editions, 2024. | Summary: "A spry collection of poems reflecting on art, the aging body, and the experiences of a lifetime"-- Provided by publisher.
Identifiers: LCCN 2023058946 (print) | LCCN 2023058947 (ebook) | ISBN 9781571315748 (trade paperback) | ISBN 9781571311559 (ebook)
Subjects: LCGFT: Poetry.
Classification: LCC PS3612.E528 T56 2024 (print) | LCC PS3612.E528 (ebook) | DDC 811/.6--dc23/eng/20240108
LC record available at https://lccn.loc.gov/2023058946
LC ebook record available at https://lccn.loc.gov/2023058947

Milkweed Editions is committed to ecological stewardship. We strive to align our book production practices with this principle, and to reduce the impact of our operations in the environment. We are a member of the Green Press Initiative, a nonprofit coalition of publishers, manufacturers, and authors working to protect the world's endangered forests and conserve natural resources. *Time Remaining* was printed on acid-free 100% postconsumer-waste paper by Friesens Corporation.

In memory of Tom Lux,
who said, "I've been writing odes."

Gratitude to B. H. "Pete" Fairchild
and William Fisher, Neruda scholar.

And to
Pablo Neruda
of course.

Contents

II. PRAISE SONGS

III. ODDITIES, AMAZEMENTS

EPILOGUE

An aged man is but a paltry thing,
A tattered coat upon a stick, unless
Soul clap its hands and sing, and louder sing
For every tatter in its mortal dress.
—W. B. YEATS

And your very flesh shall be a great poem.
—WALT WHITMAN

Look, we are not unspectacular things.
We've come this far, survived this much.
—ADA LIMÓN

As an artist, when you get to a certain age
you feel free to fool around.
—GARY SNYDER

FOREWORD

Body Odes

At the reading, Tom Lux (of blessed memory) gruffly
introduced himself, head down, dark hair slicked back and
chopped. "I've been writing odes," he said, and began.

I was thrilled not only by Lux's brilliant odes that day, but
because I too had been "writing odes." A flood of them—
unstoppable, often to parts of the body, in a form strange
and new and exciting to me, filled with surprise and delight.

My poetic life had been focused for nearly two decades on
reproducing the compact *shih* form of the ancient Chinese
poetry I loved, in which the poet says everything he knows
about a subject in eight lines, more or less. My technique
in those days was to throw out everything but the arc to
the flash of insight, mimicking the architecture of the
Chinese form.

Yet I had long loved Pablo Neruda's *Odas Elementales*
addressed to simple things like socks or salt, poems of
praise that spilled down the page, cascaded in great, narrow
leaps like a waterfall—say Angel Falls in Yosemite—
the conclusion seemingly dictated by an exhausted pen
colliding with boulders below.

Then I attended a lecture by a prominent collector of
Nerudiana, who informed his listeners of a surprising
detail. Neruda had a friend who owned a newspaper in
Caracas who told Neruda he would publish his poems but
only if they fit the width of a newspaper column! So that is

how our beloved Nobel Prize-winning poet invented the long, narrow form of his astonishing odes! I delighted in that discovery!

The next day I had a nasty bike wreck. Tore two tendons loose from my ankle that flopped over the ankle bone in a painful, debilitating dance. Lying with my ankle on ice, I found myself writing "Ode to the Ankle." Soon enough odes to other parts of the body spilled down empty pages, one after the other. I should have been arrested for having so much fun receiving and writing these poems, letting them romp. Until they came to rest in this collection.

Praise Songs
In 2002 I attended my first ever poetry workshop since resigning from journalism for the poet's path after the last of four children fledged and flew. I chose a session led by B. H. Fairchild among the many distinguished poet-teachers, not only because I admired his work but because I knew his form was totally different from mine, length his medium. He was a superb workshop leader, his reading the final night of the festival a revelation. One poem, the astounding "Beauty," required a fifteen-minute intermission! How the poet held the live audience in his hands!

The next dawn I stood in the wave break of the Atlantic Ocean mesmerized by the waves, my mind wandering to the recent death of my artist friend George Morrison. George made countless paintings of the shifting horizon from his studio overlooking Lake Superior on the Grand Portage reservation, pursuing the changing light. I found myself wondering what I was looking for. Far out under the waves my imagination called up the image of one of those invisible deep ocean creatures with frightening bioluminescent jaws. When I heard the voice in my head say, "And it is singing," I dashed back to my motel room to capture that line. But I began at the beginning, with my thoughts of George. Normally I would carve away those narrative elements, leaving only the revelatory discovery. But under the thrall of Fairchild's epic performance, I kept the story and the song, the goldmine as well as the gold. I found these longer forms worked wonderfully especially for public readings, offering listeners not only a hook but a ladder to the ear, whereas so many lyrics can speed by too fast for listeners to apprehend much aside from rhythm (why Robert Bly commonly read his shorter lyrics twice, saying the first gets stuck in the head, the second gets down into the chest). Like reading Thoreau versus Emerson, the former gives the walkabout details, the latter simply blows your mind every sentence.

Oddities and Amazements

Finally, looking in my poetry queue, I discovered that I had been writing somewhat longer poems for years, for occasions or for fun, most unpublished and gathering dust or whatever it is that writing gathers stored as digital files. And the best of them had an arc that, thanks to Neruda and Fairchild, I had grown to appreciate, one that serves listeners especially well.

Hence this collection of mostly longer poems. Thank you for listening.

JAMES P. LENFESTEY

TIME REMAINING

INVOCATION

Where Poets Go
For Richard O. "Dick" Moore, 1920–2015

The Protestant Cemetery in Rome,
tomb of Keats's bubbled blood and
Shelly's beach-scorched bones.
The couch in Oregon housing
Stafford's quiet pad, his quiet pen.
The cobbles of worn Nazareth
where Taha Muhammad Ali crafted peace
in poems inside his tiny trinket shop.
And Dick Moore's monk's cell in
assisted living in Marin, where
he knew the spine of every book
and made an eyeblind whiteboard sing
exquisite "blindness sonnets":
It is not a fair exchange, light for dark,
So much remains on the other side of light,
A world lost is never a fair exchange.

I remember digging a hole for our dog,
deep as I could among tangled cedar roots.
And my daughter could not put him in.
My wife could not put him in.
What poems he wrote with his
generous tongue.

Poets earn no better place on earth than dogs
or soldiers shot and rotting in a trench.
All get our one slim slice of soil or air,
organs plucked by condors like cello strings,

hymned by fungus, dug by moles,
a modest cloud of ragged smoke.

But listen! A poem by Sappho
was just discovered in an ancient
dump in broken Egypt!
Unfurled now from papyrus junk,
the whole earth trembled as burnished
sheaves flowered into Greek,
twice sung already in English
as the Islamic State blasts and burns
the stone remains of Ninevah.

So many fragments in the rubble—
songs sung at dawn before the battle
lost, a mother before an infant's bed,
a man incanting a lover's chin, a child
chanting charms against the dark.

And Dick Moore's suite of sonnets
arriving ten days past his death
in a book bright as Milton's
angel, a brilliant stop to time.

Tuberculosis stilled the lungs
of Keats and Steven Crane, my hero.
Seawater filled up Shelly
with cobalt blue.
Emily claimed the apt-named
Bright's Dis-ease.
And Dick Moore the final tick
of sturdy clock at ninety-five.

Some dumb thing will silence me—
a blow to the head, a drunken fender,
the creaking of the clock, bird flu.
And you?

So cobble up a shrine before you die,
a dogged hole entangled in the roots of words,
in-spire, to fill the mind with grace;
ex-pire, breath out a final song.

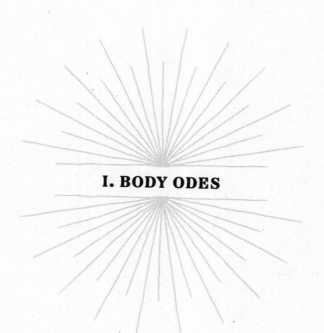

I. BODY ODES

My Left Hand

Never mind the crushed knuckle,
the one that held the nail for the hammer.
Everything you do is bent, gnarled,
upside down, devilish, illegal—
like speeding, wrong and exhilarating.

You think for yourself,
backward, from effect to cause.
You scratch up on itches, down on dogs,
stroke my beard like an absent friend,
gesticulate with forkfuls
of food, broccoli flying.
Your fingers, lazy and forgetful,
send me unzipped into the street!

How did you get so strange?
Like an elemental particle is "strange,"
a quark or boson flying everywhere
and nowhere at once,
through walls said to be solid but transparent
to your excitable turns.
You feel the world as it really is—
bizarro, curious, inelegant, unclean,
unfaithful, filled with delight.

When you were young you were restrained—
nose picker, marble flicker, ass wiper, you retired
deep into your sleeve at night, speechless.
Now you reveal your jaguar spots,
far more alert than the rest of me,

springing swiftly over the keys
ravenous for scattering prey.

You come away gripping a hairy tail in your fist,
offering up to my ears the sound you were seeking,
or a handful of feathers of the bird whose soul
you needed to possess, the bloody carcass
of a freakish longing that only you relieve,
enough red meat to spell me for a day,
though I be tarred and feathered and run out
of town by a mob of flaming right hands.

Ode to the Heart

*To be sane in a mad time
is bad for the brain, worse
for the heart.*
—WENDELL BERRY

I saw you were a good one, flapping
back and forth in the cardiologist's
scope like baby crow wings, a clenched fist,
a pelagic nudibranch self-propelled
through the dark oceanic currents of the chest.

My father's heart, and both grandfathers',
crapped out early, stress hounding them
like hounds baying a fox. Those hounds
chewed off the doors of their hearts.

Meanwhile you persist, selflessly
pumping the elixir of life,
violet in, crimson out,
seventy-plus earth years of pulse
and wave my cardiologist says
"looks good."

That cardiologist retired early,
got the hell out of the medical machine
churning out one more BMW heart attack,
to forgo the circle of Hell
called, ludicrously, "stress,"
not "murther most foul."

"Deer hart," that shameless Shakespearean
pun, bounds through the underbrush
of veins and leafy lungs, revealing
above the sternum's thin fur
the pulse of her heels,
the fatty fluff of a departing tail.

Outside, the reciprocating roar of a neighbor's
accursed lawn mower levels grass to eat the quiet day,
burning in its heart the failed guts and bones of all
bodies ever grown old, a zillion nameless dead.

Yet it too mimics the heart, back and forth,
as a motorboat labors on the lake nearby
gunning up and down the swells with
the period and frequency of a heartbeat.

Every rhythm bespeaks the Renaissance
of the heart, and before, the
langue d'oc strum of the Troubadour
before Milady, longing to hold in his palm
what he calls for her to hold in hers,
her heart, unlocked from the castle's
cage. And she lets down her
long hair, yes she does, yes she does,
and picks the lock of her maiden's door
to hold his heart in hers.
And so they die entwined, rose and briar,
sputtering valve and tenderloin,
slain by the king like pigs.

All of this misunderstanding easily erased
by a bullet to the heart,
severing the motor from the boat,
spilling gas and oil over the roiling sea,
all of us stunned stupid in response.

A boy I once knew, not
fourteen, set out with friends
to rob the corner grocery store.
The bullet he fired in panic
struck the heart, two lives lost.

The same way the heart tears open
at the final slam of the marriage door,
two hearts broken, or the phone rings
after a long night of a missing child,
the line gone dead both ends.

The heart can't take it alone.
It drags the rest of the body down
with it, the fat and the lean,
bone and gristle, air sacs and spleen,
to publicly declare its wounds
in shrieks and sobs
"wrenched from the heart."
Yes, a heavy pipe wrench
opening all the valves
of liquid despair.
Curses too, and revenge.

So cut out the heart and eat it,
"it is good," Stephen Crane said,
maybe all of us better off dragged before
obsidian knives of Aztec priests
in the end.

Unless, on a last, very good day,
it murmurs old poems and songs
learned, as a child,
"by heart."

Ode to the Belly

Hail, hail, plump paunch! O the founder of taste.
—BEN JONSON

So many want to lose you,
drop you like an anvil into the sink,
unwrap your Turkish towel covering
a sublime Greco-Roman torso!

Why is it, we wonder,
you thicken with age like curd,
like a floating, bloated goat,
like a sagging drum?

Why does the tanned leather skin
of the belt complain, like some rusted
Roebling cable holding up
an aging Brooklyn Bridge?

My hands want to play you
like a drum, a resonant bass,
slap time like a subway musician's
foot, its marvelous echo!

Squatting, we are so much more
Buddha than Jesus, bellies floating
like lotus blossoms on a pond
surrounded by waves of leaves,
riffled waters, trailing willows.

We are supposed to be as resplendent
as we are, open to sun and wind,
entirely edible in multiple forms.

My belly holds a universe of other flora
whose names I know but have forgotten,
like my kindergarten class, all of whom
are still with me holding my hand—
lovers, dancers, laggards, the fattest
the smartest of them all.

You are where the laugh lives,
the laugh that shakes the whole of us,
a quake revealing not underlying faults
but holy virtues, our ravenous capacity
for cavernous joy.

Massage

Begin with the left shoulder,
detached from the frame of the spine
but by ball, strained strings and strands,
scapula slipped toward the chest
like a sad friend longing for comfort.

On to the trapeze between
that sad, detached friend and
the neck's upright needs and desires,
knotted to keep half of us
from falling apart.

On to the wound every human knows,
the one in the geographic center of the back,
the place one can never visit alone,
only in the trusted hands of others.

Once in the center of Africa
I swam alone at dawn surrounded
by a troop of baboons,
the entire cycle of genus life
watching me idly—
grooming, grooming, grooming—
as I watched them idly,
a theater of touch,
a mantra of touch,
a museum of touch.
The back rises up in moaning
memory of so much lost touch.

For handfuls of dollars an hour
touch restored, though never
enough, never ever enough
in this long, lone human life.

Manicure

No man's hand in my ken
was ever cured by emery boards,
by buff and polish at fist's end.

No man's hand was ever sweetened
by sanding breaks and splits and hangnails
and spikes and cuticles of thin skin.

Men are cured instead in the palm,
holding therein a woman's or child's hand.
Thick palms of care-worn lines from a lifetime

of hammers and saws and trowels and buckets
of tar and rivets and wretched days on rough roofs
and under rotting houses fixing broken pipes
and on oily concrete floors wiring up
mufflers drooping from their rusty cradles.

I defend men's hands, and all the shit they
lift from manure rakes to whirring conveyors
eager to snatch away their fingers and forearms.

A man's fingertips are as sensitive as piano keys
and guitar strings, as a bee's tongue, as a spider's web.
Give them the soft touch of love and they make honeyed music.
Curl them around a handle and they will build a house.
Curl them into a ball and they can kill.

Hair

Oh great waterfall, ever
flowing, even after death,
strong and light as spider silk.

Cascading off the crags
of the cranium, over
the whorled caverns of the ears,
over beetled, furry brows to
shield the eyes from sun and
ears from wind like an electric
fence protects grazing cows.

Down over the sapling of the neck
and mossy plain of the shoulders
hiding a forest of fallen bones.

Framing the shine of the face,
eyes and cheekbones and smile
in a gilded ornate baroque frame,
a simple steel Scandinavian frame,
a Chinese black lacquered frame,
a knobby branch baobab frame.

How humans love each one of you,
building shops on every corner
with sharp beaks for plucking
and snipping and shaving and incising
and curling and straightening and braiding
and waxing and volumizing and tinting and

streaking and conditioning and dying and slicking
with fat and grease and flouncing with combs.

So many combs, earliest of human artifacts,
now stuck in towering afros, hidden in purses
and pockets, lost in car cracks and cushion folds.

And brushes! How many pigs plucked for stiff bristles
to sleek the luster and enrich the blood of the head,
rubbed and smoothed and rubbed and smoothed,
and when dying with cancer, wigged.

Never mind the musical *Hair,*
this is no story of rebellion nor claim
of independence but of *de*-pendence,
a paean to protein extruded from the
thin mantle of scalp into the volcanic
life flowing around us.

And though monks do without, and Michael Jordan,
the rest of us sail our resplendent domes
into the rough seas of morning shining
highlights into the eyes of passing barques
filled with strangers primping at the oars to dazzle us.

Ode to the Ankle

I have seen you flayed on the doctor's chart,
complex as a mountain range, fields of
vetch and poppies between white water tendons
streaming over boulders of mobile bones.

It was when the accident freed two tendons from their prison,
a life sentence, how they frolicked over the ankle bone
like snakes making love, slithering back and forth,
shameless in spring sunlight.

Until now, I stood on you like an emperor,
oblivious to the mob below the castle wall,
the ten toes and twenty-six bones,
everything multiplied, all of it holding
me relentlessly erect, greater than any ape.

Now, humbled by your rebellion,
your angry stab of pain tearing you open to the world,
swelling that distant region with soldiers
living and dead, I stand lame and halt,

wondering if the surgeon's guillotine awaits
beyond the icy prison cell, the ragged stack
under my lifted foot, the vicious boredom of the
remaining family of the body.

Or if I can rule the court again, racquet
in my hand like a scimitar, shouting orders:
IN, and OUT, and GOOD, GOOD, good,
and see again my skidding faults, and yours.

Oh ankle, to think how long the emperor
ignored your richness, your plenitude,
and to love now not one but two,
a matched pair, like emerald earrings
dripping from the lobe of each pendulous calf,

the calf I raised since a boy with admiration,
took to the state fair for judgment,
to the football stadium, the swimming hole,
exposed on moonlit summer nights,
turned this way and that, as if they
magically floated me off the earth.

While the holiest work was far below, silent,
where the ends of the tendons and raw
meat meet, the levers of the mass of all of me
springing me forward into the light.

Integument

What a marvelous wrapper,
snug even between toes!

It shines in the sun
and breathes like a forest
as if the hairs were fir trees
and the skin a swamp
with roots below water
allowing the whole earth to live
in its breathing.

And when slashed with a knife,
it glues itself back together
leaving only a nick or a road
and a story.

Covering up every sin,
every broken heart,
every living love,
every word unspoken,
every song unwritten,
every ugly thought,

while perspiring the work
of the hunt and the gather of roots
and the digging of graves and the raising
of shrines.

Whose idea was it anyway to cover
up this perfect covering, filled with

functions and history and signals,
a Great Plains of skin
harboring thatches of fur like
cottonwoods in the washes?

And yet we look down on the
coverings of our fingers as we type
poems and memos and screeds
which speak more about hangnails
and headlines and lost loves,
while the skin holds everything in,
final barrier between the messy
ooze of us and the sharp rocks
of the world, which, if
they breach,
it heals.

Hyoid

*The horseshoe-shaped bone situated in the anterior
midline of the neck between the chin and thyroid
cartilage, attached to no other bone.*

Speak to me, bone,
of floating.
You alone of all bones,
like a modern phone
unhooked, held
by your horns, a
roped calf, bawling.

Floating in the throat
like a boomerang,
holding up the tongue
like Atlas,
holding down the larynx
like Jacob wrestling
the angel.

Above you only
solid skull,
dumb as stone,
and flapping jaw,
claiming credit
for everything
you do.

As you,
lonely hyoid,

capture
and mold
the wind.

Without you
not even God
can understand.

Jaws

I watched them
in the Greek restaurant,
a roistering redolent room
where a horror show of jaws
moved up and down like dippy
birds or pump jacks,
pulverizing romaine and onions
and feta and kalamata olives (pits
deftly separated from meat with
speechless tongues),

while I, awaiting a table,
spectated this feeding frenzy,
whole tables ringed with mouths
spraying oil and vinegar,
scattering rice, tearing
skewers of limbs of lambs,
stuffing every-
thing, everything
into face holes dark as caves.

A hole in every face,
roughly in the middle,
some highlighted with lipstick,
some behind lattices of beard hair,
but still a hole, dark and fathomless.

I thought of the Buddhist
notion of nine holes, nine,

the integrity of the integument
pierced at birth by two
eyeholes, two noseholes,
butthole, pee hole,
and only the fontanel, the spirit
hole, the door of perception,
the gateway to heaven, the angel
hole, later closed up tight,
while the others, the dark ones,
open for a lifetime
like some seedy bar in Las Vegas.

And all I really wanted entering
It's Greek to Me on Lake Street
and Lyndale Avenue in Minneapolis
was my own Greek salad
with some skewered baby sheep
to feed me before the play at
The Jungle Theater next door.

But as I waited I dwelt on holes,
a dwelling so oft ignored,
I consoled myself, had I not
strolled in, alone, a hungry hole
in the middle of my
inconsolable body.

I should end there. But
did you notice that the census
of holes came up short, ears
the only two that vibrate with erotic,

vocative pleasure at songs and poems,
and when actors play someone other
than the ravenous holes they played at dinner.

Time Remaining

But with a spirit all unreconciled
Flash an unquenched defiance to the stars.
—ADELAIDE CRAPSEY

"Draw a clock," the nurse said.
Draw a clock? A clove? A pitcher
of cream? A bath? Me? I am NOT
going to waste my Time Remaining

drawing something I have known
since the first blink at my mother's wrist,
and every day on strangers, cops,
starlets, kids. An insult to be asked
to draw a clock. OK,
12, 3, 6, 9, 12, that's all
I'm giving up of Time.

But you with your doe-eyes
wait above your chartreuse mask
and burned brown skin and
patient poise and so I pencil
in the remaining numbers.
As you turn away, you note:
      "Forgot the ten."

Forget the ten?!?!
Fingers, toes, the base of
all our daily toil, no way
I forgot the ten! I abjure it!
Descry it! Deny it!

As for the three words you asked me to remember,
one was "finger," a part of the body, touch and feel,
the rest abstractions, Latinate, hookless and feckless,
like "awesome," I grant them no space.

Inside the rock-solid skull of me
lies an ocean where whales glide
and sport and sing dream songs,
And I'll be damned if I care
about a high school wall clock
in my allotted Time Remaining
in this wet and circular life
to draw tiny magnetic bits as if I were
not already high as a kite this morning
driving to the checkup because the snow
from the mountains finally arrived
as flakes big as feathers like those
dropped by the Cooper's hawk
into the backyard tearing the breast
of a fresh kill sparrow from the
arborvitae, tree of life, just yesterday,
bloody snowflakes floating down
in shared animal astonishment.

At my age I will NOT be
pinned to the cold glass face
of a kindergarten clock! (Though
I cherish my grandfather's pocket
watch, it ticked like a heartbeat
until it died in my arms.)

The Tongue Is a Smart Muscle

Think of drinking. You can't think it.
Yet using the soft velar glot
of the throat as anchor, the tongue
easily slaloms cool pools
toward burning emptiness
to slake the screams of cells
surrounded to death by salts.

It licks your lips, and hers, and elsewhere,
better, some say, than anything,
and sticks itself into space in firm contempt.

Lying in wait, lying, it will do anything,
say anything, when called upon,
with or without rest, or love, or song.
Yet the tongue plays so often innocent,
as when you sleep, or dream, or die.
Finally, no last words.

Ode to My Excellent Teeth

After reading of Coleridge's bad teeth

My ancestors—omnivorous,
long-jawed predators—
crushed the mini skulls
of idiots and fools with wisdom
teeth, that's what they're for.
Then grazed on fruits and roots and seeds
to feed delicate browsing day
among the thorns of rasp and rose and blue.

How my stalactite incisors long to seize
the flight of plentiful birds, soar them
over the undulating landscape of the tongue
to animate the cave of heaving breath
with the soaring sounds of heaven.
Without which we are but a gurgling babe
at the hard knot of the breast, a slave to love.

Today at dawn I brush them forgetfully
with cheap Pepsodent, buck a tube,
the scent of childhood running in the streets,
and climb the stairs to my lair
to write this ode, and wonder
if anything I've ever done or
will do will endure as solid artifact
in a decaying wilderness of words.
Or only the ceramic solidity of you,
plus the handiwork of a dentist I once knew.

A Memory in the Body

South Luangwa National Park, Zambia, 2000 CE

How little we know our own spines.
—SU LOVE

The guide, a chain-smoking,
drunken white racist from Malawi,
took a wrong turn in South
Luangwa National Park and stuck his
Rover to the axles in a swale of mud.

We were looking to see leopards,
abundant here, who break
the necks of prey by leaps
of stealth six feet away,
then lounge in treetops,
heavy-lidded observers
of feeble thin-skinned idiots
stumbling humbly from their
protective stuck steel shell.

In thick mud studded with lion
prints, each pad big as a silver buck,
in a glade of mopane trees,
hard as steel, splintered by elephants,
maybe the same ones we saw earlier
stomping their jumbo hassocks
with irritation at the sight of us,

he wheezed and sweated in the mud
under the Rover with his insane cig
habit and inadequate screw jack—
no highboy, no radiophone,
no water, no water at all—
with sharp U-bolts hugging the axle
aimed directly at his colluded heart—

and I entered the dreamy satisfaction
of his death, and planned my escape
through the teeming veldt,
a naked, upright, righteously pissed off
homo sapiens defended solely
by a sharp mopane splinter in my paw.

I entered a landscape fled
millenniums ago, not hunter but prey.
And as I imagined my walk
and my thirst and the thin fur
of my shirt, I grew the spine
of an older, forgotten self,
full of bluster as a young
elephant waving his ears,
tall as a giraffe,
snarky as a warthog,
proud as the pride of lions
seen yesterday devouring
.a beast twice my size,
licking their bloody lips.
Given over to no certainty

where the road led, humble
and unafraid.

On the last screw of the jack,
the car broke free.

Ode to the Inner Ear

For Scott King, poet, publisher, entomologist

My friend, felled, spent
seven days grasping the rug
of the whirling world,
tangled in the swirling
desolation of vertigo,
vomiting vanished gravity,
some dark spell
cast upon the inner
ear.

Sent by the Devil himself
to untrue the arrows
of sweet-tipped
sound emerged
from his lips
as song.

His ear among all ears!
Deft to the touch
of a poet's fit
of phoneme/
morpheme
to the
trembling fluid
of the mouth's
flute.

And none hear so clear
as he the flower
fly's buzz inside
the divine cosmos
of the garden.
No ear more
delicately tuned.

And so the Dark God Virus
singled him out, like Job
prostrate before an
unimpeachable President,
to be endured until, cured,
upright once more, facing
the sun's slant rays,
he sets and sings
the words
the whorls of his ears
justly align. As the
whirling world
rights itself
in time.

Ode to Groaning

Song of failing time,
screech of stuck limbs,
rasp of joints, slog of
flaccid muscles, rise
with moaning exhalations
of stupendous effort,
satisfied discomfort,
slowly lower into the driver's seat
with its tangle of pedals,
up onto the treacherous curb,
heave from the soft couch,
settle hard on the kitchen chair,
roll out of the tangled bed
like a pine log felled in
the forest catastrophe,
pull at socks on distant feet
stubbled with cramped toes,
tipped with razor blades,
hips set in concrete
grinding into soft legs
of elusive distant pants.

And so to groaning!
Entitled, allowed,
this pleasure of
venting oneself
unto oneself,
in the company
of oneself,
precariously

mobile,
free as yet
of attendants,
diapers,
drool.

Simian/Cetacean Me

I begin to notice the simian skull,
the dark vein splitting the forehead
eager to overflow, the white mane
hanging like a draft horse's tail,
a Percheron, white with gray spots, or
gray with white spots, the sunken eyes,
as if burrowing back into the dark
pool where damp memory lies,
aqueous humor hardened to a scum
of presbyopic melancholy, thin
wrinkled parchment collapsed
against geologic cheekbones,
only the beard mildly optimistic.

Nothing sanguine about this faded
map, only *terra incognita* waiting
over the stooped curvature of a horizon
populated by giants and dragons.

And yet I am happy as a clam,
opening and closing my watery jaws,
oddly eager for the lonely voyage
with my cetacean ancestors back into
the dark folds of the ebullient sea.

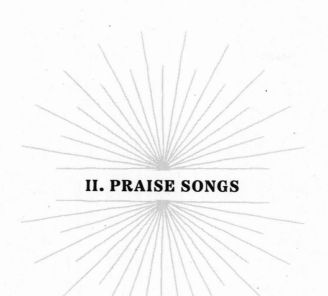

II. PRAISE SONGS

Reading Neruda Odes at Dawn

I feel a kind of shame,
listening to this largeness,
generous songs one after another
cascading down the page
like recriminations
that I did not see enough to praise,
that I did not shout loud enough
for the miners, the workers,

though I did shout for the
the fecund earth
but in squares of daily journalist
prose collapsed into the dump
or igniting small fires in the cabin,
shredded newsprint whose dark
headlines recede daily into the past
like footfalls of marching solders
back into the earth, igniting nothing
in the human heart to unbreak
the branch before heaven,
the fertile branch of plum
and cherry and orange.

My God how we have forsaken you
for the corruption of impermanent ink,
abandoned astonishment
for the plow of extraction,
tearing out your hair to rust
the dawn with fire.

I am exhausted with reading
Neruda's odes,
his generous lips and belly,
his radiant open palms
pulling up his violent socks,
shaking his salt, fingering the
womanly curve of the spoon,
the manly curve of the fork,
the smooth neck of the
carafe of wine.

Nothing left to do
but give,
and give again.
Let me leave nothing
on the plate
of this life
but crystals
of salt.

Gratitude to FOXP2

Gene once thought to express human speech.

Let's talk.
Let's talk fire.
This fire.

It has a crackling voice.
A singed skin voice.
A dripping fat voice.
A firecoal flicker,
gashed gold vermillion voice.
A dark light voice.
A mumble of embers.

From the coals, heat.
From the flames, light.
From the fire, food.
From the food, talk.

Next to you, bodies
squatting on mats of fur
encircle burnt stones
as children crawl
toward the flickering light.

We who do not speak
must watch them burn.
We who bear the gene
for speech can save them.

As they will save us every day
with syllables of sound expressed
as sense to pay us back for
ten thousand years of vigilance.

Ode to the Sound of "N"

Language is fossil poetry.
—RALPH WALDO EMERSON

Splice the sound "n" into "etymology"
with only a small discriminating pressure
of the tongue at the intersection of the hard
palate and the solid ceramic blocks
of incisors, adding a soft low growl
in the wolf of the throat,

and we veer away from the history
of the constellations of words swirling
like nebulae inside the dark linguistic
universe of our mouths where a comet tongue
like a fiery eel carves distinctions from icy light,

to change the direction of history
into living bees swarming the tops of trees,
and butterflies, my God, butterflies, how did
their impossible body plan arise?
And ants! Do not forget industrious ants
who inspired tireless Edward O. Wilson
as a boy to see in their persistent trails
the intersection of all the living
universe, how it tunnels together.
And termites with their wizard enzymes,
digestive paths harder to mimic
than modern science once supposed.

This massive meaning built into
the small of it, these two clusters
of linked sounds separated by a muscle
slickly pressed when called
to change the scale of the universe
from lost to vast,
world with an "n,"
amen.

Love Letter

For Peter Kramer

I love you, letters.
A, simple-minded ox
upside down, rolling in the hay.
B, a sideways house of
two capacious rooms sheltering
the sounds Alpha and Beta in Greek,
opening up the full Roman abecedarium
that I was taught to make with
building blocks of graphite lines,
then curves of winding cursive trails
of bottled ink.

To think, no, to imagine
the C to be a gold-
fish bowl spilled, without its goldfish;
D a pregnant doe without her head or tail;
E a sideways glance at
the channels of a labyrinth,
F an unexpected opening,
G a complex curve initiating God,
H the bar hung between two struts
that together hold up Heaven.

Ahh, letters, you swim before my eyes
from Phoenician fact to flights of fancy,
make every human sentence proud
to be writ clearly, up or down.

And so, my love, I raise my capital I,
tip it toward the goblet of capital U,
believing in, no reason why,
divinity—Alpha to Omega to the question Y.
Every letter to the hooks and beaks and claws of Z
begins with my love for the curve of U.

Ode to the Independent Bookstore

For Louise and Sue and David and Hans, et al.

Friends, if I may digress for a moment
from reciting my life's work from between
these thin, stiff covers, to look around.
Every one of these slim slabs, these
foliated bricks, these heavy letters,
these unique arrangements of runic marks,
these alphabets of lifetimes,
these categories of experience—
Fiction Memoir Travel History Mystery
Romance Adventure Poetry—
every inch-thick upright brick contains
the history of a human soul.
And I'm sorry but TV does not,
my iPhone does not,
Google does not, Google who replaced
in a historical nanosecond three librarians
working for me in my old life and faster
by one hundred thousand nanoseconds, is free
of human soul,
the soul inhabiting these bricks.
Just crack a cover, a cover at random,
see the light pour out,
starlight, sunlight, dirty bare bulb electric light,
LED light, soul light, which means also
darkness, murderous despairing darkness,
blackness within blackness,
the dripping water at the bottom
of the well darkness,

the moss-covered crumbling walls
slipping under fragments of torn
fingernails attached to broken bones
and bleeding bodies darkness,
and above always that round circle
of soul light, always and forever
known, the fontanelle of light,
the bare ruined choirs of light,
the intimation of immortality
light, the moment-just-before and
the moment-just-after death light,
each brick of a book hiding its light
between the thinnest skin of paper,
spread pulp from dappled forests.
the Pulitzers and NBAs and Nobels
may hold more light, even the most light,
but all are radiant on these walls of upright
bricks assembled one by one by the trowel
of the singular mad focus of one human life,
probably to the exclusion of spouses, children, amigos,
to the failure to fully sell one's soul in that other
marketplace, the one of things, this the marketplace
of soul things, and I fall over my thickened tongue
and cracked and bleeding cheeks and running
eyes and broken, beaten feet and
spastic, waving arms and fingertips
emitting sparks of fire
to thank you for building this
illuminated, illuminating house.

Ode to My Paper Mate Flair

I buy you by the dozen, the box,
more than French fries, than socks,
though the permanent ink
inside you has slimed more
shirts than red spaghetti or wine.
It's your drag on the grain
of the sheet that I need,
the stroke clear and bold
like platoons of Chinese
carving memory stones
or oracle bones.
You are key to the lock
of my liquid emotions,
my guide on the Silk Road
and wind-ravaged oceans.
You're the end of confusion
and all of my ruses,
my cane, my walking stick,
my sandals, my hat,
my clothes, my senses,
my football, my bat,
your blade cuts the bedrock
where all lies lay bare,
the terror of honesty,
impossible to share
without you,
my tongue,
my Paper
Mate
flair.

The Sound of Struck Wine

I love the sound of struck wine
glasses, bowl to bowl,
tantric ding and hum when
waved before an audience
of eager ears!
Stems of tall lilies fused
to blossoms of light
and heat and air and
sand from the Sahara
blown in from
unremembered age.
Cheap thrill!
Hoisted to the light
they glister and glisten,
refract and reflect,
goblets of nose and desire,
twin damsel flutes,
transparent ringing choir
of cup struck on cup,
bowl on bowl, we howl
with the buzz of it,
lie down in the grass of it,
fall into the sea of it,
swim into the space of it,
climb into the tree of it,
sing into the face
of it, music of the
spheres borne on
coils of the
inner ear

down toward
oceanic memory,
our forgotten
watery self,
buoyant swimmers
in the singing sea.

Rembrandt's Reds

For Zara, who taught me

Four colors only:
bold black,
chalk white,
blue for veins,
red for hats
and ribbons
and blood.

Lucretia
breaks the heart.
How right, my daughter,
to worship at the altar
of this painting, to see
and know grief
in its marble column of light.

Did Rembrandt paint it in a single day,
his heart breaking, as is believed,
his common law love driven
from his house by harridan Puritans?
Sacred light bathes her forehead,
fathomless despair darkens her
distant eyes, her mouth abandoned
into corners above the slant
white cut of the knife,

blood
run

down
her
thin
chemise
like
com-
munion
wine.

The Panic of Electronic Things

Push "print" and wait. And wait.
And wait for the whir and urge
and suck of paper, itself a miracle,
8.5 x 11 inches, precise as Chinese
stone walls, themselves miracles of mallets
swung by millions of expendable arms.

Worried, like waiting for a child crossing
the street alone the first time,
father glancing up from the workbench,
mother down from the desk, the
street a deep river, breath held
until the boy strides up over the bank,
feet draining into the grass.

The blank sheet sucks suddenly
into interior darkness to be struck
with the pitch-black buzz of
justified lines of letters, each
a cuneiform once carved on clay,
stamped on pallets of jugs or vellum,
runes carved on sticks,
inscriptions chiseled on stone.

Now before us thin words appear
ordered one after another, arrangement
made from the ashes of a million
campfires, so many failures of the hunt,
arms bloody but unbroken,

the spearpoint held,
tell the story, tell them all.

And so we worry until we hold
the steaming paper in our hands,
right words in right order tracked
down through ancient dreams,
no substance at all, yet solid food.

Overwhelmed with gratitude
we repeat our silicon grace:
Thank you, Mr. Hewlett.
Thank you, Mr. Packard.
Thank you, Woz.
Thank you, Steve.

Ode to the Family of Crow

I love your language
spoken in the woodlot
behind the house,
clack and purr,
growl and hum and moan.

Behind the window screen
that separates us forever,
you click and coo to babies,
yell to teens, "Tell us,
tell us, tells us
where you are."

How smart you are!
You learn our language,
feast at the wheels of our cars,
know when the garbage is out,
know when we sleep,
how angry we are,
if we own guns.

Black as starless night—
not even the blackbird's yellow eye,
the snowy egret's yellow foot—
your slick feathers eat light
like an oil slick eats light.

As a plane falls from the sky,
you fall from the sky, a shroud.
Carrion delight at your arrival,

only the living dart and complain.
Like night, you own half the world.

I have come to love all of you,
rowing your darkness at dusk
in flocks across the winter sky,
roosting as a thriving city in a
neighborhood of barren trees.

For Women Who Love Ice

For Patricia, who grew up on skates,
and took my wife by the hand
around islands and under bridges.

For Martha with her hockey stick
out there with the guys under lights
banging off the boards and ripping the net.

For Amy, whose day job affects
the whole earth, who glides at night
over black ice in reverie and no fear.

For Jan, whose racing blades
cross one over the other,
hands clasped behind, wishing
she were who she is now.

For Sue, who fell in love with her body
at the community rink—every winter
when it was flooded she became herself,
the person she has looked for ever since.

For Grace, who twirls alone.

To the Guys Who Work Outside

The meteorologist, surrounded by fake flakes
of studio snow the size of goose down, shows
off the map behind him blue with Arctic cold,
the whole week not above nine degrees.

Yet right at eight the Carhartt men arrive,
Daffy Duck boots thick with insulation, thin
gloves so fingers can handle tin snips,
they climb swaying aluminum ladders

and soon a power saw cuts new gullies
for new downspouts as old shingles fly
like scabs, tar steams in pails, and a new
sheet metal cricket silences leaks two
decades old in the abandoned chimney.

Adding another generation to the life
of a hundred-year-old house, so when
the current inhabitants are wheeled
down the sturdy stairs for the final
exit, the real estate agent will say how well
the owners maintained this place, how they
repaired the old leaks of a century past,
really buttoned it up.

But I will know it was the men in Carhartts
in bitter cold who did that work, who made the future
snug with the smoke of their breath and the scritch
of ladders leaning on the old house as they climbed.

Al's Dead

Al's dead.
He of the NRA belt buckle and
war bride who owned no shoes
'til twelve, their daughter
an MBA in finance, son a drunk.

Al's dead,
skinny as a heron,
regular at the VFW
when not working on
the house he built,
the garage he built,
the shed he built
attached to the garage,
the shed attached
to that.

Al's dead,
and the woods
are quieter now,
his hunt ended,
deer, caribou, musk
ox, moose, calmer now.

His last moose straddled the Canadian border
like a colossus, looked back at Al
with moosey disdain, jaws dripping wet weeds.
Al felled him with a single shot, field-dressed
and packed him out as 200 pounds of meat
and another 150 of head and antlers

slung a trip or two over his skinny spine,
no room now in the garage for the car.

Al's dead,
and the musk ox
in Alaska that charged
him now speaks his language,
the only language Al knew well:
moose, deer, musk ox, caribou.

His war bride retired,
the children shun the woods
like the rest of us
for the house and the bar.

And the awe that was Al
has gone, hunting on
a northerly breeze.

My New Car

is black, the oily sheen of bear
escaping through roadside grass.
I didn't want the black one
when the old white one crapped out,
but one the color of flax,
with earthen flanks, a car of
fields and roadsides.

But the darkness wanted me, as
when the bear wakes and snuffles
beady-eyed through the clearing,
fearing nothing,
the night over him open
and pure,
not black at all, but radiant
with the sheen of starlight.

Grandchildren awaiting my visit
will be surprised to be hugged
by a bear arriving in the night,
hungry for grubs and sweets,
ransacking the entire kitchen.

I stretch and snuffle.
Only five more hours to drive
and more black night ahead.

Only Cherries

Homage to Kenneth Patchen

Suppose red lights don't mean *Stop* but *Go*,
branches high off the ground exploding
with cherries, a fireworks display of cherries
against the green canopy,
the alluring voice of cherries rocking
back and forth on invisible stems.

Family voices say *Stop*,
too high to climb for a boy,
the rough bark of *No*
tearing at fingers,
the whip of thin branches,
the greedy, careless face

climbing high enough
to see over the orchard,
houses and hayfields
to the shimmer of lake beyond.

And though you grow old,
gnarled, splayed and barren,
you will never come down without
tongue crazed with forbidden fruit,
hands red with the tartness of cherries.

What I Am Looking For

My friend George Morrison, artist,
after he retired from teaching, spent
the last decade of his life in his studio
on the north shore of Lake Superior painting
the horizon. He painted hundreds, maybe
thousands of horizons. I have been in a gallery
surrounded by them, each one different
as he tried, and failed, to capture the light. Each
painting a failure, costing the rest of us hundreds
and thousands of dollars so he could keep on trying,
and failing, until he died at his easel with Lake Superior,
his divine bafflement, a line of shifting colors
outside his plate glass window.

I thought of George as I stood in the wave break
of the Atlantic Ocean at Del Ray, watching the waves
roll in, one mountain range after another in predictable
periods, unstoppable and forever,
yet each one different and impossible.
I stood gazing through the clear windows of the waves,
seeing the world below, shifting shapes of sand,
shells of living things, maybe a fish,
a pompano, in and out of sight.

Out past the yachts and fishing boats and tankers,
where sand gives way to darkness, at a depth
and pressure only imaginable, there
is what I am looking for. It is luminescent,
its shape ravenous and terrible.
And it is singing.

Like George, I too keep at it, keep peering
into the waves, listening, trying to capture
the rumble and wash with a frail net of words.
I scratch out failure after failure,
the shells of the living and dead,
tufts of feathers like sails, debris and shadows,
through dangerous offshore currents in which you must swim
sideways for your life, gulls overhead screaming
for you to give up, to fail utterly.

I lay out in the waves, arms wide, listening,
as their heft shoulders me toward shore where
the white steeple of the Presbyterian Church stretches valiantly
heavenward between the Marriott hotel and stacks of condos.
I emerge from the deep dripping with fluid,
past a pregnant mother holding a frightened child.
I see spread over the beach before me radiant children
digging their way back toward the darkness.
They are glistening.
And I am singing.

King James

*Fat enough, his cloathes being ever made large
and easie . . .*
—ANNE OF DENMARK, WIFE OF JAMES I

Namesake! How I hated your silly reign,
your lazy corpulence descended upon me
as I was young and easy under the apple boughs,
freighted with your common name.

And yet, you birthed the King James
Version of our English-speaking ways,
"The wisest fool in Christendom,"
maintained the golden age of plays.

So I forgive that you denounced
the writings of your teacher, George
Buchanan, Scotland's smartest man
(and my mother's family name!),
childe poete, actor, scholar,
playwright, tutor of Montaigne,
translator of the Psalms, author
of *Offerings of the Rustic Gods*
and of a book so good you made it flame!

For you remain the King that made
the ancient Hebrew Bible sing in English,
pleasing God's ear and mine own, and
for eternity the swollen lips of Southern
babblers and the congressman who testified,

"If English was good enough for Jesus Christ,
it's good enough for me." The good ol' KJV.

Crowned king (of Scotland) at thirteen
months, me crowned your name at birth,
my reign too now trundles to a close, my
offspring, rhymes and off rhymes, trailing
radiant plumes (to quote, who else, myself),
a "large and easie" girth settled like a swale
around these latest riddled years. As I lie lazy
in the leavings of an orchard's russet dreams,
the songs your psalms sing thrill my failing ears.

III. ODDITIES, AMAZEMENTS

After the Springsteen Concert

Because I am a man who craves quiet,
adept only at strumming the air guitar,
I did not want to go.

Yet tonight my ears ring with the memory
of standing for hours in cavernous darkness
howling with nineteen thousand other members
of the band, leaning in, full-throated,

as mighty Atlas trod in black the ashen
boards of the fiery stage, the weight of the world
emanating from his radiant crags.

Like Zeus, he struck us over and over
with lightning and peals of rolling thunder
until we stumbled out into starlight,
stunned, buzzing and bell rung.

As if we had entered chambers of the heart
as corpuscles in service to the body,
each offering our own voice
as part of the much larger sound
ringing the arena with howling wind
of song before which
pine forests kneel,
dunes sculpt ancient hills,
wave after wave of rhythm foams
in white over the rocky shore.

An arena heart so huge its pulse
changes the course of rivers and tides,
raining sweet liquid and solid salt

over the dripping tongues of all who at least
once take out their earplugs and stand up,
repelling the heartbreak of darkness.

Dawn from Tower View

Anderson Center at Tower View, Red Wing,
Minnesota, October

While I wait for dawn from the top of the tower,
Highway 61 moans its tired song through the dark.

So many stars overhead. Are they real,
or painted by the artist's hand?

Before the sun rises, how lonely it is.
My flashlight illuminates only a book
and a mind hemmed in by dew on panes.

Who told me to arise in darkness to snatch
the moon and planets before the sun wakes up?
And why is she not here with me?

I read Chinese poems and a haiku or two.
Why didn't I win that book award, I wonder?
I told some of the truth, same as other writers.
Still, the sun refuses to rise at my command.

Is that a donkey I hear braying in the distance?
Or only an ass scratching itself with a pen?

Dawn from Tower View glows slowly
through dew-streaked glass, the sun taking
its own sweet time to clear away
the razor moon, the planets one by one.

The last planet, bright as a headlamp,
cries out before it too succumbs to Dawn's
heavy hand cradling fresh oranges.

Me and my book watch as leaves appear
in waves and birds awake, beaks chattering.

A silver milk truck, gathering light,
grinds its gears onto the highway,
six of ten wheels touching the pavement.

More farmyards ahead for him,
Holstein mothers groaning in stalls
while I loiter with ink and pen.

Farmers will feed eight billion today.
How does my work compare?

So much corn growing along the road to Red Wing—
impenetrable walls, sweeping quilted hills.

Soon as the sun burns dew from rustling stalks,
harvesters like jousting knights will charge
back and forth between silos, lances flashing.

Like Don Quixote, I'll watch from the ancient tower,
retired from battle, Dulcinea resting,
queen honeybee in her nearby hive.

I'm loony as a monk illuminating sacred texts,
one letter at a time, no hurry, like the lazy sun.

Thirteen Ways of Looking at the Sun

Fusion reaction: hydrogen to helium.
How simple you are: two plus two equals one.

I watched the sunrise with binoculars.
For an hour luminous green spots decorated the ground.

Horizon, placid lake or haggard mountain,
dawn treats all equally, a democrat.

I do not know which to prefer,
the sun's light on my hand, or the sun's warmth,
the quiet of dawn, or just after.

The bird did not look like a crow carrying
a bucket of gold on its back. But it was
a crow. It's always a crow.

When I am blue like the sky, the sun
is feeding half the world. When I am dark,
the sun is feeding half the world.

In binoculars this morning, the sun became Saturn.
Not the god but the rings, the storms.

Clouds have a habit of covering the sun
like nuns, fire hidden, halo radiant.

Overhead, we forget you, like a hall light
left on. Only if you burned out
would we consider change.

Sunflowers follow you around
more than people do—spring break,
a two-week vacation.

When you leave us for the day,
the applause is deafening, waves
on a seawall, hoots of aroused owls.

Why is it so few speak your true name:
Eater of Darkness. Savior.

How do I tell you I saw God this morning?
The sun, frail and trembling through a net
of cloud, showered upon us light
enough to feed the multitudes.

Drosophila

How many drosophila do we
consume with our breakfast fruit,
those pinhead helicopters rising
over the raspberries picked last week
that I am eating right now?

Hovering over the section of lime
forgotten by gin and tonic drinkers
late in the evening, but not by you,
already laid and fecund by morning.

And bananas! Beloved Cavendish,
sweet crescent moon of potassium,
all drosophila all the time
once the skin spots brown.

When I worry about the world—
Father Sun rising hot and angry,
how we fail to care for Mother Earth
in the hospital with a killer fever,

to those parents we are pinhead bugs.
And though our Mother still loves us,
and hugs us, and gives us greens to eat,
and wild meat when we wanted,

even she, weakened, doffing her white hat
in surrender, begins to feel that the bugs
crawling all over her body, making her ill,
are not worth even the energy to swat.

Homo Homini Lupus

In college I fell in love
with the impressionism
of Georges Rouault,
his pseudo stained glass
impasto like cathedral
windows, especially
the image of the hanged man
in a landscape of savagery
and fire, the inscription:
homo homini lupus,
"Man is wolf to man."

Now that I am old, and the wolf proven
a better friend than most, the
good it does cleaning up our mess,
damaged deer devouring the forest browse
like plagues of dustbowl locusts.

And as I now see the clear-cut
that was my path, behind me a swath
of trampled grass and homeless game,
that childish word for wildlife one eats
only if one solves their ancient riddles.

And as I have now heard the chorus of the wolf
at home in the wild world, over the horizon
as the sun set, polyphonic orchestra,
and howled back my thin, sad note of longing,

desperate facsimile, inviting the pack
into the glow of my fire to ward off
the terrible predators of my kind.

Four Retired Schoolteachers from Carolina Visit Robert Frost's Grave in Vermont

As I trod the gravel path past Old First
Congregational Church toward that fearsome
litany carved on his granite slab,

there stood four white pillars above which
soared the maple tree that carries him into wings
and spirals every spring, that drips today
with the surprise of last night's rain.

"What do you know of the deaths, these four
young children chiseled here?" asked the first
who said she had studied at Duke with Randall
Jarrell, Frost's friend and critic.
"They fed each other's grief," the second said.
("Depression," she muttered, "but I hate that word.")

I know little of his life—a dozen poems and
a few wise words stored in me to mark my way,
several become clichés: "No tears
in the writer, no tears in the reader.
No surprise in the reader, no surprise in the writer."

But I had read about his second son's
quick taking by the cholera at three.
And knew well that impatience to get on, get on,
to make it someone else's bitter tale.

The brash one, tall from Carolina mountains,
said she learned through decades
of experience you can't teach writing.

"You're wrong," I said. "You can't teach
perseverance like that lying here.

But how to build a paragraph, make
a sentence work to its intent, sometimes
make sound honor sense, that can be taught,
and must be learned."

We exchanged addresses. She will write
to me which daughter was the suicide,
which merely died before her time,
one twenty-nine, the other thirty-eight.

But I think I know now why this poet's
"lovers' quarrel with the world"
was bitter, building walls of stone
in life, not mending them.

A melancholy man does not
scramble over boulders such as these,
but carries them in his pockets to the world,
to trees, a wife, the nearest
child, who steal your life away
from the private cavern of your need
to carry on.

Four Pulitzer Prizes, quiet fellowships
in shingled cottages, honorary degrees,
no praise enough.

When the wind in '62 stole
sheaves of Kennedy's inaugural poem,

that wind was Elinor,
the poem his stony own.
The nation held its breath
as he recited on, an embodiment.

As we left the grave, the quietest
of the four spoke up,
said she taught first grade,
taught children how to read!

As good a path as this one:
Acclaimed Poet, broken father.
The muse gazes up from this gray stone
toward we who wonder at persistent
beauty arrayed as mountain maples
far into Vermont.

The Terror of Publishing

What if, a thousand years from now,
the sound of that syllable fails to sing?

That line break that obsesses us,
the break between darkness and light,
the one the cop pulled us over for,
gave us a costly ticket, what if it slashes
one sound too soon?

What if the hundredth ending,
the one you finally didn't use,
was the true one, your courage failing?

What if the mother in the book
is too much like your real mother,
an angel, or not enough, washing
your foul mouth with lye?

What if that scene between father and son
is not terrible to behold, Saturn's
heat blistering the skin, but maybe
laughable, a comedy?

And the Gods you invoked
in chapter one, or in the prologue,
or the title, or in metaphor in verse three,
are displeased, surly at the nasty
twist given their rollicking ways,
so they torture you night and day

with the errors of your limited
earthly imagination?

What if the critics, of which tribe you
are chieftain, riding over the dunes
in burnoose and crop and whip,
what if they miss the point entirely,
the lance sliding by the ribs without
even a nick of skin, a drop of blood?

What if that rude flock of starlings
patrolling the lawn, freighting the breeze
with sparks of inane chatter, is my audience,
indifferent save for a bug, a worm?

Or that seagull passing by,
solitary, silent, almost elegant,
but really a scavenger, a thief,
is me, the great author,
stealing everything?

When the News Comes

The newsboy soars the heavy bag
onto the porch, and glides on.
And we are left with the despair
of our age.

Once I was one of them,
my proud head hot
with fixing the words
of the world,
fired with facts
all must know.

I love those facts still,
would give my life for them,
so few now listening,
fighting their own wars
where the news is not good,
threatening day and night.

Once I listened a whole month
to the poisonous weed of AM talk radio,
screed and rant from dawn to midnight—
fat Rush, scrawny Hannity,
smug Jason, babbling Boortz,
talking fast as they could to incite
dollars from angry ears.

I did it for you,
to tell you not
to listen.

And then was betrayed by my own,
not one question about climate change
asked of those who would be President,
as if the crumbling of the foundation
of five thousand years of the late human age
was of no interest to a bored, fatigued electorate.

And so the news keeps landing daily,
but now I want the olds,
the history plays, the Decline and Fall,
Herodotus, Darius and especially Diocletian,
the only Roman emperor ever to resign,
to raise cabbages at his castle in Split.

Of course war broke out immediately,
but he just watched from the parapets,
lip curled slightly in disgust,
but the cabbages, aahhh,
the brilliant cabbages!

Looking Up at the Ceiling After Reading "The Poetry of William Carlos Williams of Rutherford" by Wendell Berry

From the couch, I see now

the ceiling is not flat, but waves of white,
an ocean of particulate foam, a sky of shadows,

a home to surprising darkness,

as the fresh snow outside is hollowed
too with darkness, caves of silence,

as the wind of the furnace howls

and everything below the cove molding
is as if below a waterline

and the pots of narcissus and the lamps
and the chairs seem passing fishes

and the open book lies scattered along the ocean floor
like a lost ship filled with treasure

that everyone above is looking for,
that I have found.

Loaves

While I listened to the poet in the bookstore,
and commuters listened to the radio stuck in traffic,
and others fled calamity across indifferent borders,
she parked her car before the bakery next door.

As I emerged into a moist drizzle
that mirrored my melancholy mood,
she opened the hatch of her station wagon,
a Taurus, and loaded in a bag of loaves.

A bag big as a yoga ball, white
as an icecap, knotted at the top,
bulging with the round edges of
old loaves like curling stones.

She loaded another bag,
her white hair damp and short,
face clear and businesslike,
Taurus the bull strong and rusted.

I lifted the next one from the sidewalk,
surprised at the weight,
heavy as a human body,
and hefted it to her,
then the remaining two.
"For the old," she said.
"They don't have much money."

She drove off, filled to the brim with bread,
a few days old and not a spot of mold

even in the dampness of rain.
And I who already felt full inside,
yeasted by the poet's simple ingredients—
sound, sense, rhythm, and heat—
drove home in my old Subaru
said to feel like love, radio off.
And for the nonce felt no hunger inside,
nor in the world.

The Forgiveness of the Catbird

How easy you sing in the sumac grove.
How you reveal your gray black back
and shining eyes without language of rancor.

How I remember the lust I had as a boy
for guns, saving my money, loitering
around the counter at the War Surplus

until the pellet pistol was mine.
And nothing to shoot at but something
fluttering in the sumac grove.

And when you fell on your back, you
looked up at me, not dead, not alive,
and I knew I had to finish what I had begun
when I bought that gun, and never shoot again.

Now in my eightieth year,
an early riser to your melodic
mumblings outside my window,
your children, as mine, ignorant,

greeting the food of dawn with busy chirps,
mimicking other poets
who inexplicably offer songs
that try to sound like forgiveness.

Tour of Kindness

It was a dream, of course,
a tour bus coming from somewhere
to where we were, you and me, waiting,
expectant for the band, or troupe, coming from
a great distance, our anticipation, what it might be,
what it could mean, what was hoped for,
the need to name it.

And as I awoke in the fluttering before certainty,
beneath the troubled surface of the day,
the name came to me, all I remember:
"Tour of Kindness."

Now I am waiting, we are all waiting,
wondering when it will arrive,
and what it can mean.

EPILOGUE

Alone with Fire

Alone in a square kitchen
of wood and brick,
alone with fire.

A solid drapery of rain
trembles the ferns, diamond
necklaces gush from spouts.

Inside,
the poems
of Pablo
Neruda
sing to me.
So he loved Stalin too long,
I forgive him.
I forgive him his praise
too long of Fidel.
I revere him for his bees,
his salt,
his socks.

What do we have then, on a day flooded
with rain, a day in which distant islands
and cell towers disappear,
and the fluttering egos of sailboats,
and the thrum of freighters and ferries?

Warm socks, salt, and honey.
And if we gathered sticks before the storm,
enough energy to notice fire.

A hat with a brim sits jaunty on my head.
Fragrant lilacs tumble through the door.
And Pablo Neruda sits beside me,
stroking my arm.

ACKNOWLEDGMENTS

In the decade or so assembling these poems into *Time Remaining*, I have had much help. First and foremost, poet and editor Thomas R. Smith, always my first and best reader. And poet Robert Hedin for his early clear and helpful advice. And poet Jay White, who offered many useful suggestions. And Peter Kramer, architect with a good ear as well. At Milkweed Editions, editor Bailey Hutchinson, whose arrangement of the poems makes much better sense than the one I had been living with for a decade. And photographer John Walsh Jr., who asked me out of the blue to his studio for a photo session, the ones used here perfect for the spirit of this collection. And always The Anderson Center in Red Wing for its gifts of pure creative time. And Kevin Young at the Palm Beach Poetry Festival who prompted my left hand and pen to speak for themselves. And Daniel Slager, Publisher at Milkweed Editions, who again said "yes." Meanwhile, a few of these poems have been previously published here and there, including in *Crosswinds*, *Writers' Digest*, *Martin Lake Journal*, and *Great River Review*.

JAMES P. LENFESTEY is the author of multiple
collections of essays and poems, including *A Marriage
Book* and *Seeking the Cave*, a finalist for the Minnesota
Book Award. He is also the editor of multiple anthologies,
including *Robert Bly in This World*. A former college English
instructor, alternative school administrator, marketing
communications consultant, and award-winning editorial
writer for the *Star Tribune*, he received the Kay Sexton
Award in 2020 for significant contributions and leadership
in the Minnesota literary community. For fifteen years
he chaired the Literary Witnesses poetry program in
Minneapolis and led a summer poetry class on Mackinac
Island, Michigan. Founder of Poets, Writers, and Musicians
Against the War on the Earth, he currently serves on
the boards of Red Dragonfly Press in Minnesota and the
Hellbender Poetry Gathering in North Carolina. He lives in
Minneapolis with his wife, Susan Lenfestey. They have four
children and ten grandchildren.

milkweed
EDITIONS

Founded as a nonprofit organization in 1980, Milkweed Editions is an independent publisher. Our mission is to identify, nurture, and publish transformative literature and build an engaged community around it.

Milkweed Editions is based in Bdé Óta Othúŋwe (Minneapolis) within Mní Sota Makhóčhe, the traditional homeland of the Dakhóta people. Residing here since time immemorial, Dakhóta people still call Mní Sota Makhóčhe home, with four federally recognized Dakhóta nations and many more Dakhóta people residing in what is now the state of Minnesota. Due to continued legacies of colonization, genocide, and forced removal, generations of Dakhóta people remain disenfranchised from their traditional homeland. Presently, Mní Sota Makhóčhe has become a refuge and home for many Indigenous nations and peoples, including seven federally recognized Ojibwe nations. We humbly encourage our readers to reflect upon the historical legacies held in the lands they occupy.

milkweed.org

Milkweed Editions, an independent nonprofit literary publisher, gratefully acknowledges sustaining support from our board of directors, the McKnight Foundation, the National Endowment for the Arts, and many generous contributions from foundations, corporations, and thousands of individuals—our readers. This activity is made possible by the voters of Minnesota through a Minnesota State Arts Board Operating Support grant, thanks to a legislative appropriation from the arts and cultural heritage fund.

Interior design by Mary Austin Speaker
Typeset in Century Old Style

Century is a Scotch typeface originally cut by Linn Boyd
Benton for master printer Theodore Low De Vinne for use
in *Century* magazine. Later and more widely used iterations
of Century were redesigned by Benton's son, Morris Fuller
Benton, who devised the invention of type families.